ROCKHOUNDING

A BEGINNER'S GUIDE TO
ROCK HUNTING AROUND LAKE MICHIGAN

WRITTEN BY SCOT AND JENNIFER WACK

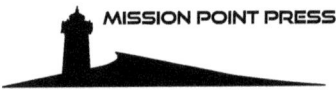

MISSION POINT PRESS

Published by Mission Point Press
2554 Chandler Rd.
Traverse City, MI 49696
(231) 421-9513
www.MissionPointPress.com

ISBN: 978-1-961302-70-9
Library of Congress Control Number: TK
Printed in the United States of America

Table of Contents

An Introduction to Rockhounding Around Lake Michigan

LET ME START BY INTRODUCING OURSELVES and share how we started looking for and collecting rocks from the shores around Lake Michigan. An activity that began a wonderful journey. An activity that has since become a happy addiction. Our story may inspire you to do the same.

My name is Scot and my wife's name is Jennifer. In the late 1960s and early 1970s Jennifer's grandfather Bob Powell used to collect Petoskey stones and polish them into wonderful carvings and beautiful pieces of jewelry. He had a small lapidary shop on the family property in Northport. He would custom-make broaches, pendants, and carvings for neighbors and visitors that came through Northport. During the summers he would sell them at art shows and rock clubs in the area.

He passed away when Jennifer was very young. Fast forward to the early 1990s when Jennifer and I first met in Maryland. One of her dreams was to live in Northport and collect rocks along the shoreline. Being from a larger city and not really sure what this whole rock collecting thing was, I agreed with her, but in the back of my mind, it was just a dream of hers. In 1993 we got married at Bethany Lutheran Church in downtown Northport.

I have to say, I was smitten, not only by my new wife, but with the area as well. We spent time up in Leelanau County doing the visitor thing, going to new places and seeing what the area had to offer. I remember going to the beach the first time. I had no idea what I was supposed to be looking for. But I knew this was something that Jennifer had great memories of doing when she'd visit the area in the summers as she grew up. She showed me her PaPa's small metal shed with grinding wheels and buffing machines and so many rocks. No one had really done anything with the small rock shop since Bob had passed back in 1976. It was like opening a time capsule. So many of his pieces were still there. Some finished, some yet to be finished. I truly fell in love with the area and really wanted to make one of Jennifer's dreams come true and hopefully one day, get to Northport to stay.

In 1998 while living in North Carolina, we decided to drop everything, throw caution to the wind, and move to Northport. We both had routine jobs: I was a carpenter and Jennifer was a nurse. We purchased her great grandmother's house just down the road from her NaNa's house and often drove to the beach to find interesting stones. There were so many colors, shapes, and sizes. I still didn't have an idea of what I was looking for, until I started paying closer attention. I've never been much of a science guy but together we started researching what we were finding. Rocks that were millions of years old. The different textures and colors. How they changed over time. Of course, Petoskey stones, Michigan's state stone, was what we sought after most. Well at least at first. Then we discovered the other fossils, Charlevoix, honeycomb corals, Cladopora, and crinoids, all living corals at one time. We learned that Michigan was once covered in a shallow saltwater environment which allowed these corals to flourish here. Then it was the abundance of other stones we could find on the beaches. Unakite, granite, agates, quartz, and more. Each stone with different colors and different mineral compositions. We learned how they were formed, either by pressure or heat or a combination of both. That was the start of something that has become very close to our hearts. PaPa's shop was there and the equipment was old so we upgraded to newer equipment and began our journey into the world of lapidary arts. We joined the local rock club and took classes on how to use the equipment we had. It wasn't long before we were cutting, shaping, polishing, and making jewelry from the stones we would find on the beach. We started going to art shows and music festivals with our craft. We were getting pretty good, although this was just a hobby at the time. As the years went by, it became more of an obsession. Off to the beach we'd go, any chance we got. Our favorite beaches were right down the road. Christmas Cove was and still is our favorite. But there was also Peterson Park, Grand Traverse Lighthouse, Cathead Bay, Point Betsie Lighthouse, Leland, and so many side road pull offs. We were always searching for some shoreline with the perfect beach.

In 2021 we decided to open a rock shop and Northport Trading Post was born. We opened the store with local goods from local crafters and vendors. We carry local honey, local maple syrup, and of course, local rocks. We brought our lapidary equipment right into the store with us. We wanted to share our love for rocks with everyone who came in. We don't have too many secrets. We'll pretty much answer any question you have about the area including where you can find the best treasures. We even started teaching classes on the polishing machines we have worked on for so long. We had finally done it. Opening the rock shop meant we could finally do what we love and share our knowledge with others. The Northport Trading Post means so much to Jennifer and me. We invite you to stop by and we can share rockhounding stories; hopefully you'll leave with more information than when you came in and maybe polish a few rocks. We hope this book is helpful to you in your quest for knowledge about the rocks and fossils in the area and how to identify them.

Good luck and happy hunting!
Scot and Jen

Tips, Tricks, and Tools

Here are a few things to consider when you think about your rock-hounding adventures.

1 Decide what your aspirations are for your trip.

What are you looking for? Do you have a certain specimen or type of rock you're specifically seeking? Do you have an endgame for what you collect? Or do you just want to find some cool stuff? Different areas around Michigan have different categories of stones. Some stones are more prevalent than others. For example, if I were looking for septarian/lightning stone, I'd concentrate my hunt to the southwest part of the state. Pier Cove and Pilgrim Haven near Fennville have an abundance of that stone. The further north you go, they are much harder to find.

2 Have a game plan.

Decide what beaches you'd like to go to and be prepared to spend some time at each. I made the mistake of heading to an area and hitting as many beaches as possible. That backfired and I was too busy rushing around to really get into my hunt.

Don't rush. Take your time. You'll be able to focus on the rocks and not just where you're going next.

3 Take an inventory of all the tools you'll need.

My go-to list consists of the following:

○ **A good rock identification book.** With this book in your hands, you're all set.

○ **Something to carry your treasures in.** A mesh backpack is great because it won't hold water and will be easy to take on and off when you need to. A lot of people take a small bucket. In Michigan, you're allowed to take 25 lbs. of rocks off beaches, per person, per year. That's a lot of rocks.

○ **A good sturdy scoop is a must.** You can either make your own or purchase one from a local rock shop or online. It will allow you to reach a little further out or go a little deeper in the surf. Choose your scoop wisely. A heavier duty scoop with teeth will let you dig a bit and pull up those larger stones. A smaller scoop is good for small stones from the shoreline. Whichever one you choose will definitely save your back from unnecessary strain.

3 Take an inventory of all the tools you'll need.

Continued from page 9

○ **A change of clothes!** Yes, it happens. You'll most likely go too deep and get wet or get hit by a rogue wave by surprise. It's a real bummer to be wet all day if that wasn't your intended outcome.

○ **If you're looking for UV reactive stones at night, make sure you have the proper wavelength UV light.** The most common wavelength is 365 nm. There are lots of UV reactive stones on the beach. Also take heed, a regular flashlight for safety reasons should be carried as well.

○ **Consider carrying a bathyscope.** What the heck is a bathyscope? It's a container that has a clear bottom. It allows you to see the rocks under the water with no wave disturbance. Mine is a 3.5-gallon bucket with a piece of plexiglass in the bottom. It's a game changer for the die-hard rockhounder.

○ As always, safety first. **Be sure to bring a good first aid kit**, some food, fresh water, charged cell phone, and a few towels to dry yourself off. I'm constantly getting wetter than I planned.

○ **Always take a buddy with you.** It's a great way to spend some time with a friend. But if you must go alone, let someone know where you'll be and what time you plan on returning. Some beaches are really rocky. One slip and you may be in a bad way, quick. Better to be safe than sorry.

4 Go That Extra 50 Yards!

The shoreline can change from week to week. One day the rocks will be as far as you can see. The next, all you see is sand. That's normal. Due to weather and water levels, all beaches have their own look and feel. Sometimes the treasures you'll find will be plentiful. Sometimes not. It's usually a roll of the dice when you try a new spot or a trusted treasure trove. You never know what you're going to find on the shoreline.

Best advice I can give is to go that extra 50 yards where other people stop. Take an extra half an hour and go somewhere no one goes. That's where you have the best luck. Beaches can be overcrowded with all the good rocks already picked over. A good storm will usually replenish them. And pay attention if you're behind someone. They may miss something. Or maybe they're not looking for what you are. I can't tell you how many times I follow people and come up with some great stuff.

And by all means, take your time. If you travel too quickly, you may miss some of the smaller specimens.

5 Roadside Pull Offs

Roadside pull offs have the ability of getting you some great finds! They're less traveled than the well-known or advertised beaches. End of county roads are also often overlooked as shoreline entryways. Some of my best finds were at an accidental or newfound spot at a pull off or end-of-road access.

Don't trespass on someone's property to get to a beach. But if there's a public access, there's no harm in giving it a shot.

6 Winter Rockhounding

Winter rockhounding can be just as fun as summer treasure hunting but you'll need a little more protection from the elements and should do a few things differently. As always, you should never go alone. One slip on the ice and a sprained ankle is not a good position to be in. Always let someone know where you're going and when you'll be back. Keep dry for as long as possible. As soon as you get wet, that's the end of the trip and time to get back to a dry, warm environment. A rock isn't worth your safety.

Don't trust ice shelves. They're unpredictable and apt to give away quickly. My favorite time of year for rockhounding is early spring when the ice is melting from the shoreline. It's usually been a few months since anyone has been out and you may be the first one seeing what the lake has to offer after a long winter of being frozen over.

Even in Michigan, you also have to think about quicksand. Well, it's not really quicksand, but can act like it. When there's ice on the shoreline, the waves continue to come in. That water hits the ice and is forced downward into the shore. Smaller sand particles are moved out from the force of the wave, leaving a void in the sand. It may look sturdy and secure, then next thing you know, you're waist deep in water and sand, another inconvenient situation to be in. Please be careful at all times. The shoreline can be a place to get out and enjoy what the lake has to offer, but always know your surroundings and take heed to all precautions. Most of all, have fun!

7 Do Research

Do your research. Go online. Join some rockhounding groups. Ask questions. Listen to the experts. Most people will share their tips, tricks, and locations for good beaches to try. There are a lot of us out here with a wealth of information. You just have to find the right person and ask the right questions.

Mohs Hardness Scale/Test

The Mohs hardness scale is a method used to determine the hardness of minerals based on their ability to scratch against each other. It was created by Friedrich Mohs in 1812 and consists of ten minerals, with each mineral being assigned a number from one to ten based on its hardness. Some stones are more difficult to test because of multiple stones and minerals with different hardnesses in their general matrix and composition, such as conglomerates, which contain different stone mix in a host matrix.

The hardness of a mineral is determined by testing it against these ten standard minerals. For example, if a mineral can scratch calcite but is scratched by fluorite, it would have a hardness of between three and four on the Mohs scale. Diamond, being the hardest mineral on the scale, can scratch all other minerals, while talc, being the softest mineral, can be scratched by all other minerals. This information is valuable in identification and in the tumbling process.

MOHS HARDNESS SCALE

Mineral Name	Scale Number	Common Object
Diamond	10	
Corundum	9	Masonry Drill Bit (8.5)
Topaz	8	
Quartz	7	Steel Nail (6.5)
Orthoclase	6	
Apatite	5	Knife (5.5)
Fluorite	4	Copper Penny (3.5)
Calcite	3	Finger Nail (2.5)
Gypsum	2	
Talc	1	

INCREASING HARDNESS

Agates

Mohs Hardness: 6.5 - 7

1	2	3	4	5	6	7	8	9	10

Agates can be found along the Michigan shoreline of Lake Michigan, while the Lake Superior agate is prevalent in Lake Superior. Agates are a variety of microcrystalline quartz that forms in cavities within rocks, often displaying color bands or patterns created by different mineral impurities. Along with their banding, they have a waxy feeling when dry.

In Michigan, agates are commonly found along the shoreline where they have been weathered and eroded from ancient basalt lava flows. These agates can range in color from white and gray to shades of brown, orange, red, and even blue and green. Each agate is unique, with its own distinct colors and banding patterns.

Once collected, agates can be tumbled and polished to enhance their colors and patterns, making them popular for use in jewelry, crafts, and decorative items. The unique beauty of agates and their smooth, polished surfaces make them highly sought after by collectors and gem enthusiasts.

Basalt

Mohs Hardness: 6

1	2	3	4	5	6	7	8	9	10

Basalt is a very common type of volcanic rock that is typically dark gray to black in color and fine-grained in texture. It's formed from the rapid cooling of lava flows on the Earth's surface. Basalt is often found in areas with volcanic activity, such as the Michigan shoreline of Lake Michigan.

In addition to their aesthetic appeal, basalt also plays an important role in the ecosystem of the Michigan shoreline. They provide habitat for a variety of plant and animal species, and also help to protect the shoreline from erosion caused by the waves of Lake Michigan.

Overall, the basalt rock formations along the Michigan shoreline of Lake Michigan are not only a reminder of the region's volcanic past, but also serve as an important and beautiful feature of the local landscape.

Amygdaloidal Rhyolite

Mohs Hardness: 5.5 - 6

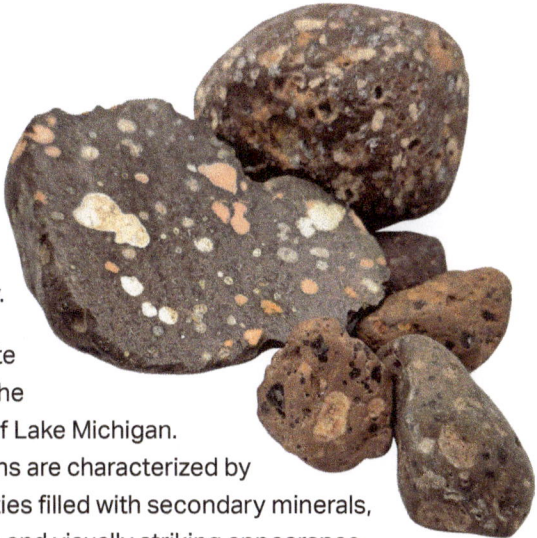

1	2	3	4	5	6	7	8	9	10

I find this one of the hardest words to say.

Amygdaloidal Rhyolite can be found along the Michigan shoreline of Lake Michigan. These rock formations are characterized by their distinctive cavities filled with secondary minerals, giving them a unique and visually striking appearance.

The amygdules or fossil bubbles in the amygdaloidal rhyolite found along the Michigan shoreline may contain a variety of minerals, such as calcite, quartz, zeolites, or others, depending on the specific geologic conditions in the area. These minerals can add interesting colors and textures to the rock, creating a beautiful and fascinating display along the shoreline.

The presence of amygdaloidal rhyolite along the Michigan shoreline is a result of the region's volcanic history. Millions of years ago, volcanic eruptions in the area produced lava flows that eventually cooled and solidified into basalt rock.

The formation of amygdules within the basalt occurred as gas bubbles were trapped in the lava flow and subsequently filled with minerals during the cooling process.

Porphyritic Basalt

Mohs Hardness: 5.5 - 6

1	2	3	4	5	6	7	8	9	10

I remember this one by saying porphyritic basalt has no pores. I've also known these as flower stones. Porphyritic basalt is another type of basalt rock that can be found along the Michigan shoreline of Lake Michigan. This type of basalt is characterized by large crystals, known as phenocrysts, that are embedded in a fine-grained matrix called the groundmass. These phenocrysts are typically made of minerals such as olivine, pyroxene, or plagioclase.

The presence of porphyritic basalt along the Michigan shoreline indicates a history of volcanic activity in the region. The larger phenocrysts in the rock formed deep within the Earth's crust or mantle before being brought to the surface during a volcanic eruption. The finer groundmass surrounding the phenocrysts solidified more rapidly at the surface, resulting in the distinctive texture of porphyritic basalt.

Porphyritic basalt rocks along the Michigan shoreline may exhibit a range of colors and textures, depending on the specific mineral composition of the phenocrysts and groundmass. These rocks can provide valuable insights into the geologic processes that have shaped the region over millions of years.

Beach Glass

Mohs Hardness: 5 - 7

1	2	3	4	5	6	7	8	9	10

Beach glass, also known as sea glass, is weathered and frosted glass that is found along shorelines where the glass has been tumbled and smoothed by the waves and sand over time. It's often found on beaches along bodies of water where glass bottles, jars, and other glass items have been discarded or lost and eventually broken into small pieces.

Along the Michigan shoreline of Lake Michigan, beach glass can be found in various colors and shapes, ranging from clear to green, brown, blue, and sometimes rarer colors like red or orange. The glass fragments are usually smooth and rounded, with a frosted appearance that makes them distinct from newly manufactured glass.

Collecting beach glass has become a popular activity for beachcombers and collectors, as each piece of glass tells a story of its journey through the water and sand. Some people enjoy using beach glass to create jewelry, art, or other crafts, while others simply appreciate the beauty and uniqueness of these weathered treasures.

Charlevoix Fossil/Favosites

Mohs Hardness: 3.5 - 4

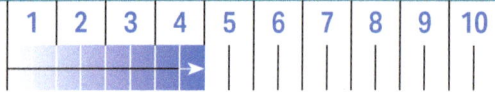

1	2	3	4	5	6	7	8	9	10

Charlevoix fossils are fossilized remnants of ancient marine life that can be found along the Michigan shoreline. These fossils date back to the Devonian period, approximately 360 million years ago, when the region was covered by a shallow saltwater sea. Smaller tubules of the coral make it distinctive from the Petoskey stone. If you think of a handful of pencils, the eraser side is larger and more like the Petoskey stone. The pencil tip side, with small heads, are like Charlevoix/favosites fossils.

Fossil hunting is a popular activity for visitors to the Michigan shoreline, as the area offers opportunities to find well-preserved fossils embedded in the rocks along the beach and in the cliffs. Local shops and museums may also showcase collections of Charlevoix fossils, providing further opportunities to learn about the region's geologic history.

Chain Coral/Halysites

Mohs Hardness: 3.5 - 4	1	2	3	4	5	6	7	8	9	10

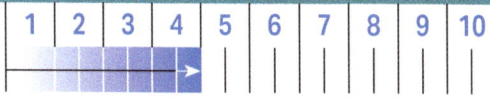

These unique fossils are my favorite to find. Chain coral/halysites are extinct fossils that are roughly 400 million years old. They evolved around the Michigan area when the state was covered by a shallow sea. This coral is very recognizable due to its chain-link raised marks formed by tubes where jelly-like polyps resided. Although fairly rare, there are certain areas more prevalent to find the coral. A great find for any rockhound!

Chert

Mohs Hardness: 7

1	2	3	4	5	6	7	8	9	10

Chert is a type of sedimentary rock composed of microcrystalline quartz. It's commonly found along the Michigan shoreline, particularly in areas where ancient geologic formations have been exposed. Chert can vary in color, ranging from white and gray to brown, black, and even red, depending on the impurities present in the rock. Chert also has a waxy feel to it when rubbed with your fingers.

Chert can form through the accumulation of microscopic silica (silicon dioxide) particles in marine environments over long periods of time. In Michigan, chert deposits can be found in sedimentary layers that were once part of ancient seas or ocean beds. Through the process of diagenesis, these silica particles can gradually lithify and solidify into chert rock.

Along the Michigan shoreline, beachcombers and rock collectors may come across chert pebbles and nodules that have been weathered and eroded from the surrounding geologic formations. Chert is known for its hardness and durability, making it resistant to weathering and erosion, which allows it to persist in the local landscape.

Chert has been utilized by indigenous peoples and early settlers for various purposes, including toolmaking and as a raw material for making arrowheads, knives, and other implements. The presence of chert along the Michigan shoreline serves as a testament to the geological processes that have shaped the region over millions of years and provides insight into the natural resources that have historically been important to human populations.

Banded Chert

Mohs Hardness: 7

1	2	3	4	5	6	7	8	9	10

We call these "Stripeys" or Zebra rocks. So many cool colors and patterns in the banding are typically caused by variations in the deposition of silica-rich materials over time. These variations can result from changes in environmental conditions, such as fluctuations in the availability of silica or the presence of other minerals that influence the color and texture of the rock. Different from agates, chert is not translucent.

Banded chert rocks found along the Michigan shoreline may exhibit bands of different colors, such as white, gray, black, brown, or red. The contrast between the bands creates an eye-catching pattern that makes banded chert a popular choice for collectors and enthusiasts of unique rock formations.

In addition to its aesthetic appeal, banded chert can offer insights into the geological history of the region. The banding patterns in the rock can provide information about past environmental conditions and processes that influenced the formation of the chert deposits along the shoreline.

Blue Chert

Mohs Hardness: 7

1	2	3	4	5	6	7	8	9	10

Not to be confused with Leland blue slag, the blue coloration of blue chert is often the result of the presence of trace elements or impurities in the silica-rich material that makes up the rock. These impurities can react with the silica during the rock's formation process, resulting in the striking blue color that distinguishes blue chert from other types of chert. A telltale giveaway for blue chert is its waxy appearance. Also, no gas bubbles, like in slag.

Blue chert rocks found along the Michigan shoreline may vary in color intensity, ranging from pale blue to deep, rich shades of blue. The coloration can be enhanced when the rock is wet, adding to its visual appeal and making it a sought-after find for rock collectors and enthusiasts.

Cladopora

Mohs Hardness: 3.5 - 4

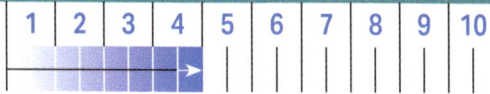

1	2	3	4	5	6	7	8	9	10

Cladopora fossils are a type of fossilized coral that can be found along the Michigan shoreline, particularly in areas with limestone rock formations. Cladopora is a genus of branching colonial coral that existed during the Silurian and Devonian periods, approximately 400 to 500 million years ago.

Cladopora colonies are characterized by their branching structures, with individual coral polyps living in interconnected tubes or branches. When these corals died, their calcium carbonate skeletons accumulated and fossilized over time, creating the cladopora fossils that can be found in the rocks along the Michigan shoreline.

The presence of cladopora fossils provides valuable insights into the ancient marine ecosystems that once thrived in the region. These fossils serve as evidence of the diverse and abundant marine life that inhabited the shallow seas that covered the area hundreds of millions of years ago.

Collecting and studying cladopora fossils can be a rewarding experience for both amateur fossil enthusiasts and professional paleontologists. These fossils offer a window into the past, allowing us to learn more about the evolution and biodiversity of marine organisms during ancient geological epochs.

Cold Water Agate

Mohs Hardness: 7 - 7.5	1	2	3	4	5	6	7	8	9	10

A cold-water agate (CWA) is an agate that can be found along the Michigan shoreline of Lake Michigan and Lake Superior. Cold-water agates are a variety of microcrystalline quartz that forms in concentric layers within cavities in rocks such as volcanic basalt. CWAs are characterized by their unique and vibrant colors, ranging from icy blues and greens to purples, grays, and whites.

The formation of CWAs are a result of volcanic activity and geological processes that occurred millions of years ago in Lake Michigan as well as in the Upper Peninsula of Michigan. As lava flowed and cooled, cavities or vesicles were formed within the basalt rock. Over time, silica-rich groundwater seeped into these cavities, depositing layers of quartz that eventually solidified into agate.

Conglomerates/Puddingstone

Mohs Hardness: 6.5 - 7.5

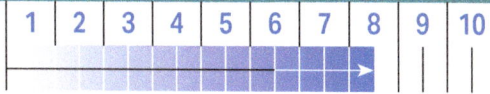

1	2	3	4	5	6	7	8	9	10

Conglomerates can be found along the Michigan shoreline, particularly in areas where ancient geological processes have deposited and transformed sedimentary rocks. Conglomerate is a type of sedimentary rock composed of rounded pebbles and gravel that have been cemented together by a matrix of finer-grained material, such as sand, silt, or clay.

In Michigan, conglomerates along the shoreline may contain a variety of rock fragments, including quartz, granite, basalt, and other types of rock. These rocks were likely transported and deposited by ancient rivers, glaciers, or other geological processes, where they were compressed and lithified over time to form the conglomerate rock.

Conglomerates/Puddingstone

	1	2	3	4	5	6	7	8	9	10
Mohs Hardness: 6.5 - 7.5										

Continued from page 27

Puddingstone, also known as plum puddingstone, is a unique conglomerate rock that can be found along the Michigan shoreline, especially in regions near the Great Lakes. Puddingstones are composed of various rounded pebbles or cobbles embedded in a matrix of finer-grained material, such as sandstone or siltstone. The pebbles within puddingstone can vary in color and composition, giving the rock its characteristic appearance resembling plum pudding.

In Michigan, puddingstone is often associated with the glacial deposits left behind by the retreat of glaciers during the last Ice Age. As the glaciers moved across the landscape, they picked up rocks of various sizes and compositions, which were then deposited in layers of glacial till and sediment. Over time, the pressure and cementation of these sediments formed the conglomerate rock known as puddingstone.

Puddingstones found along the Michigan shoreline can contain a mix of different types of pebbles, such as quartz, red jasper, chert, granite, and other rocks. The colorful pebbles create a distinctive contrast with the matrix material, making puddingstone a visually appealing and unique rock formation.

Don't be fooled by concrete or asphalt that may look like puddingstone or conglomerate. If you look closely, the matrix has a much coarser grain and will usually scratch very easily.

Crinoids

Mohs Hardness: 3.5 - 4

1	2	3	4	5	6	7	8	9	10

Crinoids are marine animals that belong to a class of echinoderms and are commonly found as fossils along the Lake Michigan shoreline. These creatures are also known as sea lilies due to their appearance, which resembles a plant or flower. Crinoids have a cup-shaped body attached to a stalk, with feathery arms extending outward to capture food particles in the water.

Crinoids were abundant in the ancient oceans that covered the region that is now Lake Michigan during the Paleozoic era, millions of years ago. When these creatures died, their calcium carbonate skeletons accumulated on the ocean floor and were eventually preserved as fossils in the sedimentary rocks of the area.

Fossilized crinoids can be found in limestone and shale formations along the Lake Michigan shoreline, particularly in regions with a rich geological history. These fossils often resemble delicate star-shaped patterns or segmented stems, and their intricate details provide insights into the ancient marine environments and ecosystems.

Collecting crinoid fossils along the Lake Michigan shoreline is a popular activity for fossil enthusiasts, paleontologists, and beachcombers. The fossils serve as valuable artifacts that offer a window into the past, showcasing the diverse marine life that inhabited the area millions of years ago.

Epidote

Mohs Hardness: 7

1	2	3	4	5	6	7	8	9	10

Epidote is a green semiprecious mineral that can be found in the Lake Michigan area. It's usually stringy in appearance and very green, particularly in association with a rock known as unakite. Unakite is a type of metamorphic rock that consists of pink feldspar, green epidote, and quartz. It's abundant in the Great Lakes area, although usually secondary to a host mineral.

Epidote can be found in small crystals or as massive aggregates within the unakite rock, creating a unique and beautiful color combination of green and pink. This makes unakite a popular choice for jewelry and decorative purposes.

Feldspar

Mohs Hardness: 6 - 6.5

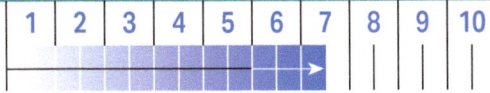

1	2	3	4	5	6	7	8	9	10

Feldspar is a key component in many igneous rocks, such as granite and gabbro, and can occur in different colors, including pink, white, and gray. These rocks can be seen in various formations along the Lake Michigan shoreline, adding to the natural beauty of the area. It's best known as the peachy pink in unakite and granite.

Fossil Soup

Mohs Hardness: 3.5 - 4

1	2	3	4	5	6	7	8	9	10

The term fossil soup is used to describe the vast array of geological materials that can be discovered by beachcombers and rock collectors as they explore the beaches of Lake Michigan. This includes a variety of fossilized marine organisms such as corals, brachiopods, crinoids, and trilobites, as well as rocks like agates, chert, conglomerates, and more.

The diverse mix of fossils and rocks found in fossil soup reflects the region's rich geological history and the unique deposits left behind by ancient seas and glaciers. Fossil soup provides a treasure trove of natural history waiting to be explored and studied, offering insights into the ancient environments and ecosystems that once thrived in the area.

Gneiss

Mohs Hardness: 5.5 - 6.5

1	2	3	4	5	6	7	8	9	10

Gneiss is a type of metamorphic rock that is characterized by distinct banding of mineral grains, often alternating between light and dark layers. While gneiss is not commonly found along the Michigan shoreline, it can be present in certain areas where ancient geological processes have acted upon existing rocks to transform them into gneiss.

The formation of gneiss typically involves the metamorphism of prior rock types such as granite, schist, or sedimentary rocks under intense heat and pressure over long periods of time. This process causes the original minerals in the rock to reorganize and recrystallize, forming the prominent bands or layers visible in gneiss.

Along the Michigan shoreline, gneiss may be found as part of the region's bedrock formations or as large boulders that have been transported by glaciers or other geological processes. Gneiss rocks can vary in color, texture, and composition, depending on the minerals present in the original rock and the conditions under which the metamorphic process occurred.

Gowganda Tillite

Mohs Hardness: 6.5-7.5

1	2	3	4	5	6	7	8	9	10

Gowganda tillite is a distinctive rock formation with a glacial origin that has been found in parts of Michigan, particularly in the Upper Peninsula but also found in Lake Michigan. Tillite is a type of sedimentary rock made up of poorly sorted and unstratified rock fragments, ranging in size from clay to boulders, that were deposited by glaciers. Gowganda tillite specifically refers to a unique tillite deposit that dates back to the Huronian glaciation period, around 2.2 billion years ago.

The presence of gowganda tillite in Michigan indicates significant glacial activity and climate changes that occurred in the region billions of years ago. The deposit of tillite suggests that the area was once covered by ice sheets that transported and deposited the rock fragments over vast distances, forming the distinctive rock layers that can be observed today.

Gowganda tillite is recognized for its unique characteristics, including a pinkish coloration caused by the inclusion of volcanic ash material within the rock. The deposit often contains a mix of rock types, including granite, quartzite, and other materials that were carried by the glaciers and incorporated into the tillite formation.

Granite

Mohs Hardness: 6

1	2	3	4	5	6	7	8	9	10

There's so much granite on our beaches! Granite is a type of igneous rock that's typically found naturally along the Michigan shoreline, as Michigan's bedrock is primarily composed of sedimentary rocks such as sandstone, limestone, and shale.

However, granite can be found in certain areas of Michigan's Upper Peninsula as well as Lake Michigan, particularly in regions where ancient volcanic activity and geological processes have brought granite to the surface.

Granite is formed through the slow cooling and solidification of magma beneath the Earth's surface. It is composed mainly of quartz, feldspar, and mica minerals, giving it a distinct speckled appearance and high durability. In Michigan, granite deposits are often associated with Precambrian rock formations that are millions of years old.

Hag Stones

Mohs Hardness: 7

1	2	3	4	5	6	7	8	9	10

Hag stones are usually comprised of a chert mineral with a natural hole worn through the stone. They are fairly rare and considered to be lucky to the finder. They were once revered and used as amulets for jewelry purposes.

Honeycomb Coral/Favosites

Mohs Hardness: 3.5 - 4

1	2	3	4	5	6	7	8	9	10

Favosites, also known as honeycomb coral, is a genus of extinct colonial coral that is commonly found as a fossil along the Michigan shoreline, particularly near the Great Lakes. Favosites corals lived during the Paleozoic era, primarily in the Silurian and Devonian periods, approximately 415 to 360 million years ago.

Favosites corals are known for their distinct honeycomb-like appearance, with a repetitive pattern of hexagonal or polygonal cells that form the structure of the colonies. The honeycomb coral sometimes appears translucent or almost has an agatized look. These coral colonies built intricate skeletons of calcium carbonate, which became fossilized over time.

Horn Coral

Mohs Hardness: 3.5 - 4

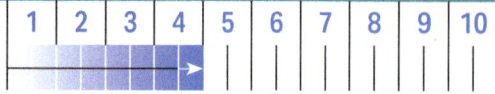

1	2	3	4	5	6	7	8	9	10

Horn coral is a type of fossilized coral that can be found along the Michigan shoreline, particularly near the Great Lakes. Horn coral belongs to the order rugosa and existed during the Paleozoic era, particularly in the Silurian and Devonian periods, approximately 415 to 360 million years ago.

Horn corals, with a long, cylindrical structure, are named for their horn-like shape. These solitary corals lived in ancient seas, attaching themselves to the seafloor and feeding on plankton and microscopic organisms through tentacles that extended from the top of the coral.

In addition to their cylindrical structure, fossilized horn corals have distinct ridges or lines running lengthwise along the coral. The fossils are typically made of calcium carbonate and can be found in limestone, shale, and sandstone rock formations along the Michigan shoreline.

Jacobsville Sandstone

Mohs Hardness: 6 - 7

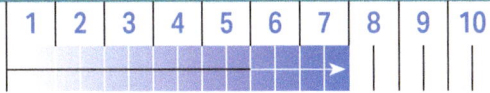

1	2	3	4	5	6	7	8	9	10

Jacobsville sandstone is a type of sandstone found along the Lake Michigan shoreline, particularly in the Upper Peninsula of Michigan. Jacobsville sandstone is nearly 1.1 billion years old. This unique rock formation is known for its striking red and brown colors, as well as its distinctive banding and veining patterns. Mined in the Keweenaw Peninsula in Jacobsville, it was shipped all over the Great Lakes.

In addition to its aesthetic appeal, Jacobsville sandstone is also of geological significance. It's known for its durability and resistance to weathering, making it a popular choice for building materials and decorative purposes.

Leland Blue Slag

Mohs Hardness: 6

1	2	3	4	5	6	7	8	9	10

Leland blue slag is a unique type of slag glass that is found along the shores of Lake Michigan, predominantly by the town of Leland, Michigan. It's believed to have formed from the remnants of iron ore smelting in the area during the late nineteenth and early twentieth centuries.

Leland blue slag is characterized by its distinctive blue color, often with streaks of other colors such as white, gray, and black. Another telltale sign of slag is small bubbles or vesicles in the material. These are cooling bubbles from when the byproduct was cooled quickly as it was dumped into the water. It's a popular material for jewelry making and other crafts due to its striking appearance and historical significance.

If you come across Leland blue slag during your walks along the shores of Lake Michigan by Leland, you've found a special and unique treasure! It's a fascinating reminder of the industrial history of the Great Lakes region and can make for beautiful and eye-catching pieces of jewelry or decor.

Leland blue slag can be found all over the shores and inland Michigan. However, the term Leland is a geographical term used for where the smelter byproduct came from. There were many smelters around Michigan and the Upper Peninsula in the late 1800s. The blue slag should always be characterized by location. For example, there was a smelter in Elk Rapids, Michigan. The blue slag that came from that smelter should be named Elk Rapids blue slag. This supports the history of smelting and smelter locations during an important time in Michigan history.

Limestone

Mohs Hardness: 2 - 4

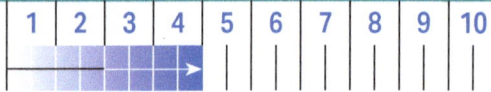

1	2	3	4	5	6	7	8	9	10

Limestone is a common type of sedimentary rock that can be found along the Michigan shoreline, particularly in regions near the Great Lakes. Limestone is composed primarily of calcium carbonate minerals, often originating from the accumulation of marine organisms such as corals, mollusks, and foraminifera. In Michigan, limestone formations are significant features of the state's geology and can be seen in various parts of the shoreline.

Limestone rocks in Michigan may appear in different forms, including bedrock layers, cliffs, outcrops, and beach exposures. The presence of limestone along the shoreline is a result of the sedimentation and lithification processes that occurred over millions of years, as marine sediments accumulated and solidified into rock layers.

Along the Michigan shoreline, limestone formations can offer valuable insights into the ancient environments in which they were deposited. Fossils of marine organisms found within limestone rocks provide evidence of the past seas that covered the region and the diverse life forms that inhabited them.

Limestone is valued for its durability, versatility, and aesthetic qualities, making it a common material used in construction, landscaping, and architectural applications. The use of limestone in buildings, monuments, and other structures highlights the importance of this rock type in shaping the cultural and economic landscape of Michigan.

Petoskey Stone, Michigan State Stone

Mohs Hardness: 3 - 3.5

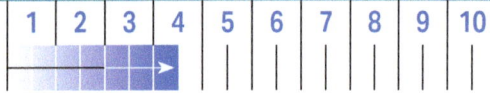

1	2	3	4	5	6	7	8	9	10

The Petoskey stone is a fossilized coral found along the Michigan shoreline, particularly near Lake Michigan and Lake Huron. It's the state stone of Michigan and is prized for its distinct hexagonal pattern resembling a honeycomb, which is created by the fossilized remains of the *hexagonaria percarinata* coral. The Petoskey stone gets its name from the city of Petoskey in Michigan.

Chief Petoskey, also known as Ignatius Petosegan, was an important leader of the Odawa (Ottawa) people in the early nineteenth century. Chief Petoskey's name translates to Rising Sun or Sunbeams of Promise, and he played a significant role in the history and culture of the Odawa tribe.

The connection between the Petoskey stone and Chief Petoskey lies in the cultural significance of both entities to the state of Michigan. The Odawa people have a deep-rooted history in the Great Lakes region, and Chief Petoskey's leadership and legacy embody the resilience, strength, and traditions of the Odawa tribe.

The Petoskey stone serves as a symbol of Michigan's natural heritage and geological history, while Chief Petoskey represents the indigenous culture and heritage of the Odawa people. Both the stone and the chief hold important cultural, historical, and symbolic meanings for the people of Michigan and the broader community.

As a state symbol and a tribute to the Odawa tribe's legacy, the Petoskey stone and Chief Petoskey continue to play integral roles in preserving the cultural identity and natural beauty of Michigan. Their stories are woven into the fabric of the state's history, reflecting the interconnectedness of geology, Native American heritage, and the land itself.

Quartz

Mohs Hardness: 7

| 1 | 2 | 3 | 4 | 5 | 6 | 7 | 8 | 9 | 10 |

Quartz is a common mineral that can be found in various rock formations and environments along the Michigan shoreline. While quartz is not common by itself, it's a widespread mineral that occurs in a variety of geological settings, including sedimentary rocks, igneous rocks, and metamorphic rocks.

Quartz may be present in sandstone rocks, which are composed primarily of quartz grains cemented together. Sandstone formations are common along Michigan's shoreline, particularly in areas where sedimentary deposits have been lithified and exposed.

Quartz can also occur in igneous rocks such as granite or in the form of quartz veins that run through other rock types. While granite is not as prevalent along the Michigan shoreline, it can be found in certain regions of the state, particularly in the Upper Peninsula where ancient volcanic and igneous activities have brought granite to the surface.

You may come across quartz pebbles, sand grains, and even larger quartz crystals washed up on Michigan beaches. These quartz specimens may vary in color, clarity, and size, depending on their origin and geological history.

Septarian Nodule, Lightning Stone

Mohs Hardness: 3.5 - 4

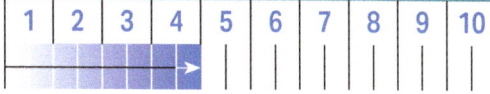

1	2	3	4	5	6	7	8	9	10

Septarian nodules, also known as septarian concretions or lightning stones, are unique geological formations that can be found along the Michigan shoreline, including at locations such as Pier Cove. Septarian nodules are rounded, often irregularly shaped structures that contain a combination of different minerals, including calcite, aragonite, barite, and occasionally other minerals such as quartz, dolomite, and pyrite.

Septarian nodules form through a process known as diagenesis, which involves the precipitation of minerals in sedimentary rocks over time. These nodules typically consist of a cracked or fragmented outer surface with distinctive patterns of mud cracks or

Septarian Nodule, Lightning Stone

Mohs Hardness: 3.5 - 4

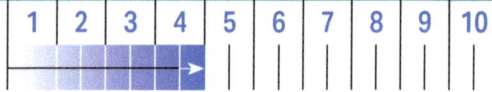

1	2	3	4	5	6	7	8	9	10

Continued from page 47

shrinkage cracks, while the interior may exhibit crystal-filled cavities, or a radiating pattern known as a septarian pattern.

The term lightning stone is sometimes used to describe septarian nodules due to their crackled appearance, which can resemble the branching patterns seen in a lightning strike. The unique colors, textures, and patterns found in septarian nodules make them prized by collectors and enthusiasts for their natural beauty and geological significance.

Pier Cove, located along the Lake Michigan shoreline in Michigan, is known for its diverse geology and the presence of various rock formations, including septarian nodules. Beachcombers, rockhounds, and nature enthusiasts can explore the shoreline to discover and collect septarian nodules, appreciating the intricate patterns and mineral compositions of these fascinating geological specimens.

Sodalite-Rich Syenite Stone/ Glowstone

Mohs Hardness: 5.5 - 6

1	2	3	4	5	6	7	8	9	10

There are multiple names for this stone. While it can be found sporadically, sodalite-rich syenite is not commonly found along the Michigan shoreline. Sodalite is the mineral that fluoresces bright orange under UV lighting. Michigan's bedrock is primarily composed of sedimentary rocks such as sandstone, limestone, and shale, as well as some igneous rocks like basalt and granitic intrusions.

Sodalite-rich syenite is an igneous rock composed primarily of feldspar minerals, with smaller amounts of other minerals such as hornblende, mica, and quartz. It's similar to granite but contains little to no quartz, giving it a different mineralogical composition and appearance. Syenite is typically coarse-grained and can exhibit a range of colors, including pink, gray, or green.

Stink Stone

Mohs Hardness: 2 - 3

1	2	3	4	5	6	7	8	9	10

Often referred to as stink stone, its actual name is vesicular limestone. They are formed near lava pits when gas bubbles are created as the lava cools and are rumored to stink when broken open. These cool stones can be found abundantly along the shores of all the Great Lakes. We've broken some open and experienced a very slight smell, in my opinion. You'll have to make up your own mind if the rumor is true.

Stromatoporoid

Mohs Hardness: 3.5 - 4

1	2	3	4	5	6	7	8	9	10

Stromatoporoids were once thought to be in the coral family although they're now classified as fossilized sea sponges. Fossilized in mostly limestone deposits, these ancient sponges appear layered from the side. Although the fossilized top sometimes resembles something like a Petoskey stone, that isn't the case. Another nickname for stromatoporoids are dimple stones, referring to the outward dimples in the top of the sea sponge.

Syringopora Fossil

Mohs Hardness: 3.5 - 4

1	2	3	4	5	6	7	8	9	10

Syringopora is a genus of fossilized tabulate coral that can be found along the Michigan shoreline, particularly in regions near the Great Lakes. These fossils represent ancient colonial coral structures that lived in the seas during the Paleozoic era, predominantly in the Silurian and Devonian periods, approximately 415 to 360 million years ago.

Syringopora corals are characterized by their cylindrical or tube-shaped structures, which consist of interconnected individual corallites that form colony structures. These fossils can vary in size, with some specimens showing intricate branching patterns and detailed structures that were once part of the coral colonies.

Along the Michigan shoreline, syringopora fossils can be discovered in limestone and shale rock formations. Fossilized remains of these tabulate corals provide valuable insights into the ancient marine ecosystems that existed in the region during the Paleozoic era. By studying syringopora fossils, researchers can learn more about the biodiversity, environmental conditions, and geological history of Michigan's ancient seas.

Unakite

Mohs Hardness: 6 - 7

1	2	3	4	5	6	7	8	9	10

Unakite is a unique type of metamorphic rock that's composed of pink orthoclase feldspar, green epidote, and quartz. It's named after the Unaka Mountains of Tennessee and North Carolina, where it was first discovered. We also refer to this stone as the Christmas stone due to its reddish feldspar, green epidote, and white quartz.

Unakite is typically found along the Michigan shoreline and can occur in certain geological settings in the state. There are areas where they are more prevalent.

Unakite forms through the metamorphism of granite, in which the pink feldspar and green epidote minerals combine to create the distinctive mottled appearance of the rock. The presence of unakite in Michigan may be associated with regional metamorphic events and processes that have affected the state's bedrock over time.

These occurrences may be rare and localized, potentially found in regions with metamorphic rocks or areas where geological processes have resulted in the formation of this unique rock type. While unakite is not as commonly associated with the Michigan shoreline as other rock types, its presence in certain geological formations adds to the diversity of the state's mineral resources.

Variolite

Mohs Hardness: 6

1	2	3	4	5	6	7	8	9	10

Variolite is a type of igneous rock that contains green hornblende or actinolite needles in a fine-grained, often porphyritic matrix. It's a rare rock type that's sometimes referred to as snakeskin due to its distinctive appearance resembling twisted cords or knots. While variolite is not commonly found along the Michigan shoreline, it can occur in certain geological settings within the region.

Variolite forms through the alteration of basaltic rocks, typically as a result of hydrothermal or metamorphic processes. The green hornblende or actinolite needles within the rock give it a unique texture and appearance. Variolite may exhibit a mottled or banded appearance, with green needle-like structures contrasting against a darker matrix. While variolite is not as prevalent as other rock types in the state, its presence in certain localized areas adds to the diverse mineral resources and geological history of Michigan.

Visual Identification Guide

Agates

Basalt

Amygdaloidal Rhyolite

Porphyritic Basalt

Beach Glass

Charlevoix Fossil/Favosites

Visual Identification Guide

Chain Coral/Halysites

Banded Chert

Blue Chert

Cladopora

Cold Water Agate

Conglomerates/Puddingstone

Crinoids

Epidote

Feldspar

Fossil Soup

Gneiss

Gowganda Tillite

Visual Identification Guide

Granite

Hag Stones

Honeycomb Coral/Favosites

Horn Coral

Jacobsville Sandstone

Leland Blue Slag

Limestone

Petoskey Stone

Quartz

Septarian Nodule/Lightning Stone

Sodalite-Rich Syenite Glowstone

Stink Stone

Visual Identification Guide

Stromatoporoid

Syringopora Fossil

Unakite

Variolite

Rock Tumbling Tips and Explanations

Rock tumbling takes your treasures from the beach and polishes them to bring out the beauty of your stones. Polished rocks can be used for a variety of applications.

Polish a large number of stones at one time and you can create so many different crafts using the stones you personally found, including jewelry. In this section you'll get an overview of the process and explanation of the differences between two different kinds of tumblers.

I'll share what's personally worked for me. There may be a tip or a trick added to my explanation as well. Have fun with it—I know I have!

I've found tumbling is a trial-and-error process until you get what works for you down to a science. Stone size and quantity, proper grit usage, cleaning between grits, spacers (when and what to use). These variables can affect the process and the outcome of your first couple of runs.

Choosing your first tumbler can be tricky. The hobby can get quite expensive quickly. I would suggest you go online and find some tumbling groups. There are many tumbling options out there. My first choice would be a single or dual drum tumbler with 3.5 lb. barrels. I'd also suggest getting graded grit and you'll want to have spacers available.

Let's talk about grit for a moment. There are four main stages that you'll run during a tumbling cycle. Stage one will most likely be 80 grit. Stage two recommends 220 grit. Stage three recommends 600 grit and stage four will be 1200 to 1500 polish. All these grits should be silicon carbide. It carries a hardness of nine on the Mohs scale and tends not to round out after use. The 1200/1500 should be aluminum oxide, cerium oxide, or tin oxide. I prefer aluminum oxide. Sometimes when you get grit, it will be labeled 80/90 or 80/120.

That's ungraded grit. That means there's some 80 grit in there, but there may also be some 120 grit as well. It's perfectly fine to use but I prefer graded grit. Graded grit has been screened to ensure all the particles are approximately the same size. So, if it's labeled as 80 grit, you know that's exactly what you're getting. Using graded grit is a personal preference for me—I want to know exactly what I'm using when tumbling.

Choosing your stones is a very important step in tumbling. It's necessary to choose like hardness stones to tumble together. For example, you wouldn't want to tumble stones that carry a hardness of 3 with stones that have a hardness of 8. The higher hardness stones will beat up and damage your lower hardness stones. They'll either wear down much faster or be crushed and disappear in the lower stages. Count your stones when you put them in the tumbler. Between stages, if your count is off, you may have a rogue stone that has snuck in.

Once you've chosen your stones, it's time to load the barrel. It's recommended that your barrel be about two-thirds to three-quarters of the way full. This allows room for the rocks to roll and move about the barrel freely. Now it's time to add the grit. It's recommended to use two tablespoons of grit per pound of rock or stone. For example, with a three-pound barrel, you should use six tablespoons of grit. I personally have better luck using a little bit less, about one-and-a-quarter tablespoons per pound. This amount may vary to meet your needs and your expectations. After you've loaded your stones and your grit, it's time to add the water. Add just enough water to cover your stones. The barrel shouldn't be totally filled with water. Again, this allows a lot of room for the stones to move freely in the barrel.

At this point, stage one, you'll want to use 80 grit which is the most aggressive. It will smooth rough edges and start the process of smoothing the stones in preparation for the next stage. For the hardest stones, stage one will require six to eight days. But let me remind you, there's no harm in periodically stopping and checking on your stones for a few reasons. The first is just a check on the process itself. Are the stones getting smoother? Have you lost any stones? Secondly, are they ready to move to the next stage? If your stones are still sharp or have rough edges, you should leave them in and check in another day or two for progress. Is your stone count still true? Are you unaware if a lower hardness stone slipped in? No big deal, it's a trial-and-error learning process. It will be okay—just make a mental note for future tumbling. Once you've determined that the stones are to your liking, you can move to stage two but there are a few things you need to do before going forward.

First, clean your stones and barrel thoroughly when changing grit. Do not dump grit down a sink or bathtub drain! I can't emphasize this enough. Doing so will clog your drainpipes and cause a lot of plumbing problems. Trust me! I suggest using a colander to collect your used grit and dispose of it outside. Some pour it in an old bucket, while others dig a hole for it in the backyard.

Most people suggest running their rocks for a few hours in a borax/water solution to make sure all of the previous grit is removed. The reason you clean your stones and barrels so well is to avoid contaminating your next stage grit. If you haven't cleaned your stones and barrel properly, the previous grit is still present. For example, even if you're ready to go to stage two at 220 grit, if any 80 grit remains, the harder grit will take over and continue to roughen your stones. This causes a lot of unnecessary frustration. It's extremely important to clean everything as best as you can. Once you're ready for the next stage, add your rocks. You may notice your rocks may not come up to the same level as they did when you started. That's because the process is working and your stones have been ground down to reveal a smoother, rounder stone.

So, what's next? This is where spacers come into play. Some people use ceramic media, some people use plastic media. I've found that plastic works best for me. And in a pinch, I go down to the local hardware store and purchase some tile spacers to use. You'll use these spacers to take up the room in the barrel that has become void because your stones have become smaller. You want your tumbler to be about two-thirds to three-quarters full. So, add your stones and fill the rest of the way with the spacers. Then, add your grit. You'll most likely be using 220 grit at this time. Like I said before, I prefer to use one-and-a-quarter tablespoons per pound. This may vary a bit as you choose what's right for you. Add your water, just under the level of what you're tumbling. Secure the top and start on your second stage.

Stage two will also run for six to eight days. Truly the process is the same as stage one. After a few days, check your process by opening the barrel and examining your stones. Are they all still there? Is it continuing to smooth and round your stones? This is where patience comes into the mix. It's very hard to wait such a long time for you to run through all the stages. Your patience will pay off! When you're ready to move to stage three, remember to clean your stones, filler media, and your barrel thoroughly. And I'll say it again, do not dump your used grit down a sink or bathroom drain. Once you've cleaned everything, you're ready to move to stage three.

Stage three is no different from the previous stages other than the grit you'll be using which is 600 grit. Once you've refilled your rocks and filler media, add your 600 grit and water. Secure the top and let it go for six to eight days. Check after a few days in to observe the process. Every stage is about the same, it's almost like a rinse and repeat process. When you think you're ready to move to the next stage, clean everything and start the process again.

Stage four is your final stage. It's also the polishing stage. This will complete the process and leave your stones with a nice smooth finish and shiny appearance. You'll complete the cleaning process as you've done in each previous stage. The polishing compound you'll use will be either aluminum oxide, tin oxide, or cerium oxide. I prefer aluminum oxide. After you thoroughly clean your stones, add them to your barrel. Don't forget your filler media. Add in a few drops of mineral oil as well. It's not necessary but it lubricates the rocks a bit. Add your polishing compound and water to level and let it run for six to eight days. Check after a day or two. Are you happy with how they look? This is where trial and error comes into your process. You may choose to shorten or lengthen the stage by a day or two, whatever works for you!

If you find your stones aren't shiny or they're cloudy, there may be a few reasons for this. Either you've used stones that aren't close enough to each other on the hardness scale or you've improperly moved your stones too quickly to the next stage. Or it may be you have inferior or ungraded grit which isn't doing the job that it's meant to do. Or lastly, you haven't cleaned your stones and media completely between stages. When this happens, and it does happen, I look at my stones to see if they're smooth enough. If need be, I'll drop back to stage two and start over. Trial and error. Don't give up! I know it can be frustrating, but you can do it. Always have fun!

Tumbling Softer Stones

As for softer stones and fossils like Petoskey stones, yes, you can tumble them as well, but the process will be a little different. Since they are only about a 3 on the hardness scale, make sure you only tumble them with other like hardness stones.

For the first stage, don't use 80 grit, it's way too aggressive, instead use 220. The same amounts apply as previously detailed above, about one-and-a-quarter tablespoons per pound. The trick is to check the process every twelve to twenty-four hours. The stones will smooth out fast and you don't want to wear your stones away. It may take thirty-six to forty-eight hours, but it will never run a full six to eight days like harder stones. When you're satisfied that they're smooth enough, go ahead and move to the next stage and use 600 grit. Make sure you use filler with your stones as they will take up less room. Once again, for these soft stones, check them every twelve to twenty-four hours. When you're happy with how they look, move on to the final stage.

For the final stage, don't run them in the tumbler, instead use a polishing compound. Take the compound powder and add some water to make a paste. Use a pair of old jeans or a felt square to hand polish the stones. They're so soft, a tumbler isn't likely to get them polished well. I've found hand polishing works best for me.

Remember, tumbling is a trial-and-error process. Don't get discouraged. If the stones come out cloudy, you may not have left them in a stage long enough, your grit may be inferior or ungraded, or there was a problem cleaning between stages. You'll fine-tune ratios as you go and make some really cool treasures. Don't forget to have fun doing it!

Another type of tumbler to consider is a vibratory tumbler. The basic stages are run the same way, four stages, all the same process. The biggest difference is that a vibratory tumbler will tend to keep the shape of your stones. A rotary tumbler will most likely round your stones.

If you have flatter or shaped stones you're preparing for a project or jewelry, a vibratory tumbler may be the best choice for you. Be careful if you use a vibratory tumbler and make sure it's for rocks. There are other vibratory tumblers available but they're for brass. They aren't watertight and will leak. Also, the springs are not strong enough to carry the weight of stones. You'll most likely find a spring on the floor in the morning, leading you to a couple of hours in clean up. I've found that out by experience and just trying to save you the trouble.

I've also been asked about noise control. A great way to quiet a tumbler is to keep it in the garage or a basement. It can be placed under a crate or in a cooler. If you choose to do this, make sure there's a bit of airflow as tumblers put off heat. Don't let it overheat and result in an unneeded fire hazard.

I hope the overview of my process helps! Now go out there and get you some rocks and have fun!

Hand Polishing Your Treasures

Hand polishing your finds can be very rewarding! You'll need a few things before you start. First, gather all your materials. Wet/dry sandpaper is a must. Regular sandpaper won't work as well as it breaks down if it gets wet and you'll be wasting money. The reason you use wet/dry sandpaper is you always want to keep your stone wet. This does a couple things. For one it will keep dust down when you're sanding. Silica dust, or for that matter any dust, is harmful to your lungs and should be avoided at any cost. There are also some stones that are toxic and can really do some damage to your lungs if you're not careful. It also acts as a lubricant between your stone and your sandpaper. The rougher grits will work best with a little help. It also keeps the stone cooler. This is just as important in your lower grits as in your higher grits when your sanding movements will become quicker and smoother.

The grits most commonly used are 80, 220, 600, 1000, and 1500. The lower the number, the more aggressive the grit is. I know a lot of people use up to 10,000 grit. I don't feel that that's necessary, but that's my opinion. You may choose to go as high as you want, personal preference. You're also going to need a good final polish. Just like in tumbling, tin oxide, cerium oxide, or aluminum oxide are good choices. My personal preference is aluminum oxide. Lastly, you'll need a buffing cloth—either a piece of felt or a small square from a pair of old jeans. Once you have everything, you're ready to get started.

Now, choose your stone. So many choices! Keep in mind, you want to know the hardness of the stone you'll be working with. This indicates how long and how hard this project will be. A Petoskey stone carries a Mohs hardness of 3. That will be much easier to polish than a piece of quartz that carries a Mohs hardness of about 7. For this example, I'll be using a Petoskey stone.

STEP ONE: I usually keep a small bowl next to me so I can dip my stone or sandpaper in to keep the stone wet. I'm going to use 80 grit sandpaper first. This sandpaper is very aggressive and is used to smooth really rough areas of the stone. If you have divots in your stone, you'll have to sand down past the divots if you want a smooth surface. After you start working with the first grit, it's going to look like you're destroying your stone. Don't panic! It's going to be okay. Keeping your stone wet, sand all the way around the area you want to polish. Just like when sanding wood, if you just go in one direction, you'll create grooves. So hit it from all directions, different angles or in a circular motion. This step is going to take some time but it's a very important step. Once the stone is uniform in its appearance, you're ready for the next step!

STEP TWO: You'll be using 220 grit. Don't forget, keep that stone wet just as you did with the 80 grit. Move the stone across the sandpaper in all different directions and angles. Sometimes it's easiest to place the sandpaper in one hand and hold your stone in the other. This allows the sandpaper to conform to your hand and will hold the rock's shape. It can be difficult if you're trying to sand on a hard stationary surface. That can also quickly tear up your sandpaper. Find what's comfortable for you. You're going to sand that stone down to a uniform look. You'll notice that the deep grooves the 80 grit left are a little more subtle. Keep that stone wet! I can't say that enough. Once you get a uniform look to your stone, you can move on.

STEP THREE: You'll be using 600 grit. This is a very important step as well. As with the previous steps, move the stone or the sandpaper in all directions. Up, down, left, right, sideways, circular, every which way you can. The important part of this step is checking your stone for scratches. There's no need to go on to the next step if there are any scratches in your stone. To check for scratches, your stone must be completely dry. If you find scratches, stay on this grit until they're gone. Higher grits tend to only aid in polishing the stone, they won't remove scratches. If you find a deep scratch and can't seem to get it out, drop back to the 220 grit and see if that helps. Remember, if you drop back a grit, you must use the higher grit to catch up with the process. Once you've removed all the scratches you should see a pretty, nice looking stone in front of you when it's wet. If it's dry, it will still be cloudy and not be very pretty. If your stone is cloudy when it's wet, most likely you haven't taken enough time on a lower grit. Stay on this grit until your stone is pretty much clear when it's wet. Once you have a uniform look to your stone and you're happy with it, you can move on to the next step.

STEP FOUR: You'll be using 1500 grit. These next grits are just as important as the earlier ones but they're going to be much easier to complete. Remember, now you're in the polishing stage. Move the stone or the sandpaper in all directions. Dry and check your stone for scratches frequently. If you find a scratch, you may elect to work a little harder on that portion or maybe drop back a grit and see if you can remove it from there.

Take your time. Don't rush through these steps. The more time and patience you put into the process, the happier you'll be with the outcome. Once you've spent enough time with this grit, you can move to the next higher grit. When you're choosing your next grit, don't make the gap between grits too high. For example, you don't want to go from 500 to 2000 grit as that will quickly wear out your 2000 grit. A gradual increase in grit is the best thing to do.

STEP FIVE: You'll be using 1500 grit up to as high of a grit as you'd like to go. The higher you go, the easier the final polish and the better your stone will look.

Remember to keep your sandpaper wet. Move your stone across the sandpaper or your sandpaper across the stone. Whichever process you choose, cover the stone from all directions. Up, down, left, right, circular motion. Spend some time, don't rush. Patience really makes a difference in your final product.

STEP SIX: Final polish! Easy peasy! You'll need that tin, cerium, or aluminum oxide. Like I stated before, I prefer aluminum oxide. On a small plate, add a little water to some of the polishing compound and make a paste. Take a soft cloth and work the polishing compound into the area of the stone that you polished. You can use felt, a piece of old denim, leather, or a polishing cloth.

Some people don't even use a polishing compound. If you take your grits to 10,000 or more, that's normally sufficient to hold a nice polish.

As for coating your stones, it really depends on what you're doing with your final product. I don't normally like to coat my stones with any kind of polyurethane spray. It will eventually break down, yellow, or chip away. If it's in direct sunlight, it will deteriorate faster. The same goes for epoxy, nail polish, lacquer, or any other spray or coating chemical.

There's nothing wrong with spraying your stones, as long as you know you'll have to clean and recoat your stones at some point.

Stones always look prettier when they're wet or polished but sometimes you want your stones to have that wet look without all the work. There are a few ways you can do this. If you want, put all your stones in a glass jar to display them. Don't use water as it will turn cloudy and algae will form in about a week or two. If you really clean your stones, it may last a little longer. Instead, I suggest using mineral oil which will leave your stone's brilliant colors and look intact without clouding up or growing algae. Don't use baby oil or vegetable oil. Those substances will break down over time and leave you with a mess trying to clean up your stones. Also, it's kind of stinky after a while.

Another idea for displaying your stones would be attaching them to a picture frame or a birdhouse. In this instance, I recommend a good epoxy resin glue. Take your time with these adhesives and abide by the cure time. If you don't, your stones may not stick or may slide off. I do recommend sealing your projects at the end, knowing you'll have to recoat at some point in time. We use a non-yellowing polyurethane that will give your stones that wet look and bring out the brilliant colors and textures that your stones offer. As always, have fun with it!

Lapidary Equipment

There are so many different types of machines out there that will allow you to cut, polish, or sculpt rocks. My suggestion would be to find your local gem and mineral society. Don't look up rock club on the internet—you'll get a whole different outcome. Sometimes a local rock enthusiast group will have their equipment set up for members to use for a fee. These rock groups are full of well-educated, willing to teach, talented rockhounders. Most of the time they're more than willing to show you the options in the lapidary arts.

We currently have a 6" Cab King and an 8" Cab King. These machines each have six different polishing wheels on them. These units are water fed by a submersible pump which we keep in a bucket underneath the work bench. It collects sediment and waste material from cutting, shaping, and grinding rocks. It must be changed out every so often so clean water is used against the wheels.

The first two wheels are solid steel. They're unforgiving and are used for grinding and shaping. The first wheel is 80 grit. This wheel is the most aggressive one on the machine and really grinds down the stone. It eliminates sharp edges and quickly gets to the bottom of any divots you may have. It may appear that you're destroying your stone. You're not, trust me. This wheel smooths the stone down to a uniform texture all the way around the area that you're polishing.

The second wheel is 220 grit and will further smooth your stone, shaping and getting grooves that the previous wheel made. Every time you move wheels you need to make sure the texture of the stone is even all the way around.

The third wheel is 280 grit. The third through the sixth wheel are a little different. These wheels have about a quarter inch padding behind the wheel. It allows you to push a little harder and keep the shape of the stone. This third wheel is very important and will be the last wheel that will change the shape of your stone. You want to move

your stone in all angles and positions. When you get to the end of this wheel, make sure to completely dry your stone and check for scratches. If you find scratches, keep working on it. This is the only wheel that will take away the scratches. If you move on to the next wheels, the scratches will remain.

Once you've verified that there are no scratches, the next three wheels are used exactly the same way. You want to spend some time on these wheels. There is no set time limit but the longer you spend on these wheels, the better your final product will be. When you've gone all the way around the stone, up, down, left, right, top, bottom, all different directions, it's time to move on to the next wheel. These final three wheels will be 600, 1200, and 3000 grit. You'll be able to feel the texture difference between each grit. After the final wheel, you're ready for a final buff.

We use a 4" bench grinder with a cotton wheel attachment. The polish we use is either Fabuluster or Zam. Be sure not to heat up your stone too much. It doesn't take long to buff your stone to a high luster. You can also use those polishes on a Dremel polishing attachment as well.

Tips on Drilling for Jewelry

Drilling your treasures can be difficult. The best advice I could give is "take your time." If you rush, even just a little, you can actually do more damage to your stone or your drill bit.

We use a Dremel press setup for our small holes. Anything bigger than ¼", we use a stand-up drill press. Granted you don't need a press system. You can drill freehand with a Dremel, controlling the bit as it goes through your stone but it's a lot easier with a press. You'll always want to use a reliable company for your drill bits.

To use a bit, you must first determine the hardness of the stone. Petoskey and fossils drill fairly easily. They're between 3 and 4 on the Mohs scale. Agates are more like 7.5 or 8 and will take longer to drill. You'll most likely go through quite a few bits by the time you get the hang of it. We buy our small bits in packs of fifty.

We always submerge our stones when we drill for a couple of reasons. First, it keeps the stone and the drill bit cool. It will also eliminate dust or debris flying up into your face. A small Tupperware bowl is all we use. But you must be able to hold that stone underwater and secure it with one hand. It's a bit tricky at first but you'll find the best position for you.

Our first step is to mark the stone with a small marker. It will help you align the stone when it's under water. When you start to drill, the piece should be steady and on a firm base. Gently tap the top of the stone to start the process. Go slow. You'll see debris start to flow out of the hole. That's good! Don't rush. In a pulsing motion up and down, lightly push the drill bit into the stone. Let the bit do the work. If you push too hard it will burn out your bit. That pulsing motion allows debris trapped in the hole to escape. If you don't clean the hole out as you're drilling, it will lessen the life of your drill bit. They like clean surfaces to drill into.

If you're going all the way through, start in the front and go towards the back. You may get a bit of a blowout if you go too fast. Or it may pop the top and now you have to fix and drill again.

Beaches and Parks List

We recommend visiting some of these beaches and parks along the west side of Michigan on your next rockhound adventure!

There are so many more—get out and explore!

- Grand Mere State Park
  7337 Thornton Dr.,
  Stevensville, MI 49127

- Rocky Gap Park
  1100 Rocky Gap Rd.,
  Benton Harbor, MI 49022

- Van Buren State Park
  23960 Ruggles Rd.,
  South Haven Charter Twp, MI
  49090

- Pier Cove Park
  2290 Lakeshore Dr.,
  Fennville, MI 49408

- Summit Park
  5581 S. Lakeshore Dr.,
  Ludington, MI 49431

- Magoon Creek Natural Area
  2925 Red Apple Rd.,
  Manistee, MI 49660

- Sundling Park
  2925 Red Apple Rd.,
  Manistee, MI 49660

- Orchard Beach State Park
  2064 Lakeshore Rd.,
  Manistee, MI 49660

- Old Facefull in Pierport
  Corner of Lakeview Rd. and
  13 Mile Rd., Pier Port,
  Bear Lake, MI 49614

- Frankfort Public Beach
  Marquette Cir.,
  Frankfort, MI 49635

- Point Betsie Lighthouse
  3701 Point Betsie Rd.,
  Frankfort, MI 49635

- Empire Beach
  10484 Niagara St.,
  Empire, MI 49630

- Leland Beaches
  Christmas Tree Beach/South
  Beach, west end of Reynolds Rd.

- Vans Beach, 205 Cedar St.
  off Vans Rd.
  North Beach, off North Rd.

Peterson Park

○ Onomonee/Gill's Pier Beach
At the intersection of Gills Pier
and Onomonee Rd.

○ Peterson Park
10001 E. Peterson Park Rd.,
Northport, MI 49670

○ Christmas Cove
Island View Dr.,
Northport, MI 49670

○ Grand Traverse Lighthouse
15500 Lighthouse Point Rd.,
Northport, MI 49670

○ Old Mission State Park
Old Mission Point,
Traverse City, MI 49686

○ Barnes Park Campground
12298 Barnes Park Rd.,
Eastport, MI 49627

○ Fisherman's Island
Bell's Bay Rd.,
Charlevoix, MI 49720

○ Magnus Park
901 W. Lake St.,
Petoskey, MI 49770

○ Wilderness State Park
903 Wilderness Park Dr.,
Carp Lake, MI 49718

Our Favorite Beaches in Leelanau County

I'd have to say our favorite beach up here to hunt for treasures has to be Christmas Cove. Just about five miles from our store, Northport Trading Post, this is the first beach we visited when we moved here. It's a long wide beach with lots of pretty rocks! We find lots of Petoskeys, Charlevoix, unakite, and so many different colors of granite. You never know what you'll walk up on. There's a steep driveway in the beginning, especially if it's busy and tight parking, but it's worth it. There are rustic bathrooms on site. There are about twelve steps down from the trail that's located at the south end of the parking lot. It's a great beach for kids to swim and explore.

Peterson Park is another favorite! Lots of parking, a great viewing deck with binoculars, and a newly installed playground for the kids. It's also a great spot for picnics. The sunsets are extraordinary! It's the steps that are going to get you: one-hundred-and-fifteen down but well worth it! The rocks are a little bigger here, so be prepared to carry up any treasures you find. There's a pavilion that can be reserved for weddings and bathrooms on site.

Gill's Pier/Onomonee Beach is our fossil beach. I've found more fossils at this beach than some of the others. A lot of Petoskey stones, cladopora, and Charlevoix. It's at the crossing of Gills Pier and Onomonee roads. Just limited parking and no bathrooms but the rocks are definitely abundant.

Leland beaches are a definite must. There are three of them. South Beach off Reynolds Dr., Vans Beach in the center of town, and North Beach at the end of North Rd. My personal favorite is South Beach; it's not as crowded as Vans although the two beaches are on the same stretch. The access points are different. Here you'll have the opportunity to find the elusive Leland blue. It's the waste product of the smelting industry. While smelting raw iron in the foundries at

Leland, slag, the byproduct of that process, was thrown off as waste. It's actually molten glass with other impurities. Some of the best pieces can be used by jewelers to create beautiful pieces of jewelry.

If you like lighthouses, you'll definitely want to stop at the Grand Traverse Lighthouse where so much history can be learned. It's also a state campground with camping sites, bathrooms, and a playground as well. The shores around the lighthouse are shallow. A lot of the stones are a bit sun-bleached but they're plentiful. It's a little harder hunt but as I always say, you never know what you'll find at the beach

Michigan Beach Walking Law

Is it legal to walk the beach in front of someone's home in Michigan?

Short answer, yes, with exception. You may walk along the shoreline of Michigan uninterrupted from the water line to the Ordinary High Watermark (OHWM). The OHWM is defined as where the movement of water creates a distinctive mark, such as where vegetation starts. You may not set up camp, put a blanket down, or loiter.

Long answer, the 2005 Michigan Supreme Court case Glass v. Goeckel, held that the public trust doctrine protects the public's right to walk along the beach. Not surprisingly, private property groups are unhappy with the decision, although the opinion is consistent with most courts' interpretations of the public trust doctrine, even on privately owned land. Lakefront property owners may own the land down to the water's edge, but the public trust doctrine nevertheless allows the public to walk on the land between the water's edge and the OHWM, the place on the shore up to which the presence and action of the water is so continuous as to leave a distinct mark.

Reference: Glass v. Goeckel
473 Mich. 667, 703 N.W.2d 58 (2005)

NORTHPORT TRADING POST

LOCAL*LAKE*LIFE
NORTHPORT MICHIGAN

We hope this book was both informative and useful to you on your next rockhounding adventure!

HAPPY HUNTING!

powered by dot.

www.ingramcontent.com/pod-product-compliance
Lightning Source LLC
Chambersburg PA
CBHW052120030426
42335CB00025B/3069